MOONFALL

Moira Andrew
&
Angie Butler

Publish & Print
www.publishandprint.co.uk

Contents

Moonfall - Poems by Moira Andrew

The First Full Moon - Poems by Angie Butler

Moonfall

Poems by Moira Andrew

For Fiona and Jen, for Norman,
for Ian and in memory of Allen

Hauntings

I hear
their haunting cries
from a darkening sky
look up,
a v-shape formation
forging
its follow-my-leader
path to destinations
known only
to grey geese
themselves.

I marvel
at their confidence
these ghosts
of autumn,
the way they
change leadership
mid-flight, their
voices cutting holes
in the air
as they disappear
into the nearly-night.

Daydreaming

Outside is where things
happen, where rain invents
upside-down mirrors, where
the sun glares, fierce
as a Cyclops' eye, where,
on cold grey days, snow
feathers the winter air.

Outside is where sky
meets fields and fences,
where rainbows splash
paint on the air, where a
meddling wind plays ghosts
in leafless branches,
drums on dust-bin lids.

Outside is where the
world starts, where, if
you're very lucky, you'll
see a squirrel parachute
from the trees. We gaze out
of the classroom window
where the outside waits.

Full moon

opens wide her arms
       hums
              a jazz standard
under her breath
       stretches
              reaching
for the highest shelf
       selects
              a silver jug
fills it to the brim
              with clear cold light
pure as mountain water
              tips it up
(so heavy, she needs both hands
       to bear its weight)
pours the see-through shine
       across
              each winter garden
sits back, arms folded,
       sings aloud
              in sheer satisfaction
       her voice
a fine high soprano
                her feet tapping
to the beat of the blues,
       the blues
              of old New Orleans

Seamstress

She pushes thick spectacles
more firmly on her nose,
chooses threads with care,
soft white, snow-white,
a vivid, almost transparent
                     pure white.

She peers at the needle,
shining silver in the light
of a winter moon, considers
the vast canvas spread below
stubbled fields, leafless trees,
                     tiled roofs.

Out of practice, it takes time
to build up the old rhythms.
Once confidence returns, she
works quickly, the in-and-out
of her needle racing to a
                     lightning flash.

Thoughts spin through her head,
how she once embroidered her way
across the countryside, dreaming up
ever more complicated patterns,
like a lace-maker, featuring only
                     white on white.

Like old times, she thinks, as the
temperature drops and she mulls
over the threat of global warming,
I'll give it my best shot! Knuckling

4

down to the task in hand, old skills
                    flood back.

Come the dawn, frost embroiders
familiar gardens, roads and houses
with that other-worldly winter magic
Beautiful, everyone breathes, mobile
cameras at the ready. Global warming
                    is forgotten

and an old lady takes a well-earned rest.

Such beauty tonight

The moon's a beauty
tonight, my friend says,
so we open the blinds,
search the night sky
anxious not to miss her.

The moon, wearing
just enough make-up
to get by, nothing flashy,
looks fabulous, smiling,
just a touch superciliously.

Nowadays she keeps
every mirror hidden away –
why? we wonder,
in our opinion, she's
as beautiful as ever.

But what with space craft,
astronomers, scientists
and general busy-bodies,
the moon's become wary
of compliments, unbelieving.

Tonight she's *The Snow Moon,*
such brilliance, such beauty.

Dragon's eye

Red, glowing,
glaring
in your direction
and you cower,
trying to avoid
his direct gaze.

Not that you
have a hope in hell,
if you're
in his sights
no chance
you've had it.

You soft-soap him,
tempting him
with compliments,
the beauty
of his rugged scales,
his white teeth.

All to no avail,
so you rebel,
mock his evil eye
and with one streak
of vicious scarlet,
he glares, just once

and blinds you.

Black lace

Winter trees,
their naked branches
writing poems
like promises
on the skyline.

Each word,
every rhyme
part of the pattern
in the intricate tracery
of pure black lace.

They hide
the new green
of spring deep
as a curtsey, a promise
in petticoats.

So we look up,
strain to read
the lines of poetry
in bare branches
lacing the horizon.

Not yet, not yet,
the poems chide,
A promise given
is a promise kept
and the branches

two-step in the breeze.

Thumbprint

A pale winter sun
smudges the skyline
just a thumbprint
         a vague impression
on the dove-grey of morning.

Snowdrops in their hundreds
         pour discreet riches
over the churchyard wall
         where winter walkers
capture their silver on mobiles.

For this hour, crows wheel
         and cry overhead,
ducks surf the brook, children
         throw bread and spring leaves
green fingerprints on the earth,

Covid fading to a mere mirage.

Dandelion

After four weeks away
we come home
to an outburst of colour,
green, green and more green
a backdrop to the blue
of forget-me-nots
of cornflowers, the yellow
of Welsh poppies, late tulips,
buttercups, laburnum chains,
to the white of spirea.

After the arid grasses
of Cyprus, its sun-soaked fields,
rocky mountainsides,
we gorge on the greens
of late spring, early summer
the exploding colour
like fireworks in our eyes.
The garden is at its best,
full of promise, majestic with
new growth, with blossom.

A lone dandelion, proud
on its dark stem, stands
to attention on the patio,
its bright head a beacon
of light, the only colour
braving cool grey stone.
Technically, it's a weed,
its delicate yellow petals
to be deplored, eradicated.
Up close, it's beautiful, just

a flower in the wrong place.

100 daffodils

They open
golden mouths,
lick their yellow lips
and purse them
into kisses
for Valentine's Day.

They glow
lighting up
the morning kitchen,
spill promises on
the breakfast table
with marmalade & toast.

100 daffodils,
(or more perhaps?)
such over-the-topness,
such glory
all saying these three
well-worn words,

I love you.

Tulips from Sainsbury's

(For Norman)

In a burst of metaphor,
(he doesn't pretend
to be a poet), he says;
They're the drama queens
of the flower world, yes?

And I have to agree, so
slim, so erect, so elegant, with
that stand-offish look, white
and yellow, purple and pink ….
yet they die with such dignity.

They open smooth petals
wide as wings, all arrogance
lost, share their innermost
secrets, show off boot-black
stamens, bend at the knees.

Like the man says, tulips
are born for the stage,
know how to turn on theatre,
reluctant to leave, they hold
open their bright skirts, wait

for applause as they curtsey
                again and again
true drama queens to the end.

Making

Well, there's making
and there's making...
soup of various varieties
is my preferred job
in the kitchen – I'm
certainly no pastry cook.

Then there's making do,
my mother's motto when
we were children, socks
darned, left-over mince
re-heated – me? I'm more
of a 'thrower-out' these days.

And there's the joy of
making free, *Take what
you like,* a neighbour says,
shaking his apple tree,
ripe fruit falling – tarts,
jam, souffles in my sights.

Making up is something
else – our faces of course –
but it's what we do
with words, drawing them
from the air as we work
at bringing poems to life.

And there's making the best
of things and making sense,
but topping everything, there's
love-making, the warmth

of a man's arms, his breath,
his lips, his mumbled words –

making doesn't come any better.

Dead bird

It lies
a bundle
of black feathers
the winter sun
catching tips
in a flash
of iridescent blue.

It lies
dropped from
December skies
feet in the air
in an attitude
of supplication
sad, so very sad.

Cat in the sun

A neighbour's cat
sits
on our garden table
in the flimsy
March sunshine
licking her fur
honing it
to perfection
just being
a cat.

So in charge
of herself,
so sure
undisturbed
by passing cars,
by tree surgeons
wielding choppers,
a vicious saw,
a stump grinder.

She's too busy
with her image
to bother
stretching lazy paws
one by one,
re-arranging her tail,
half-lidded eyes always
on the alert, hiding
a readiness for action.

She sits
on our garden table
soaking up the sun,
contented,
feigning sleep,
absorbing warmth,
her whiskers twitching,
posing
statuesque

in her sheer cattiness.

Last light

The sun dims a touch,
hard to be sure, just
a greying streak,
little more,
before a final vivid blaze,
pale pink,
      scarlet,
            royal purple.

A faint light
draws its veil
over the evening sky
a blink of the eye
and it's dark,
an all-encompassing
      thick dark,
           solid
that last glimpse
of colour
swept away
      into blackness,
           gone.

Time

holds its breath
mountains dream
seas shush,
stroking the shore
with quiet waters
and the moon
hides her silver face.

It's strange,
an unfamiliar
hesitation between
one heartbeat
and the next,
a watching world
waiting, wondering

what's to come.

Kilner jar

I store my words
in glass jars
sometimes they
wink at me like eyes.
I place them on a high shelf
print stick-on labels.
Use before sell-by-date
(but I leave the date open.)

I can never tell
when I'll need them again.
I listen to conversations,
sometimes borrow
other people's spoken words.

My pleasure, he says
not really meaning it
(although it's a nice thought)
so I gather pleasure words
fingertips
 moonstones
    seashore
      anemones
        chocolate
hoard them all
against the cold of winter
like the plums
my mother preserved
in Kilner jars.

I swore they blinked
at me from their shelf

in the kitchen cupboard.
Too much imagination,
that's your trouble!
my mother complained.

Tonight I'll upend a jar
spill words across
the computer screen,
If they gaze wide-eyed at me
I'll wait till they close,
sleep, dream me a poem.

A nice cup of tea

They tell me
I make a good cup of tea –
not that I'd know
I don't drink the stuff,
can't stand the smell,
astringent, sour, thoroughly
unappetising.

I've brewed tea
first thing in the morning
for the men in my life –
and for my daughter,
a compulsive tea-Jenny
(well-named). She takes it
milky, by the bucketful.

I remember making tea
for my mother, bringing it
to her bedside, she in curlers
and blue hairnet. She struggled
to sit up, *Thanks dear,* she said,
not knowing. I had to tell her,
Mum … Dad died in the night.

We'll meet again

So sings Vera
who died this week -
by this time no doubt,
she'll have found out
if it's true.

Not that I believe
a word of it, bluebirds
are rare in Dover and
heaven must be vastly
overcrowded.

Imagine searching
for your beloved's face
among the seething mobs -
bad enough if you
lose him in M&S.

I remember coming
to this conclusion
in my teens, just as
I parked my bike
in the cellar.

Heaven, I decided
there and then
is a complete myth.
I remember the sense
of disillusionment

My trouble with
Vera's idea of meeting

the dear long-dead
is, I'm so old no-one
has a hope in hell

of recognising me.

These were the days

Remember when melon
dusted with powdered ginger
was the height of
dinner-party sophistication?

It goes alongside the heavy
silver cutlery, newly polished,
being lifted from velvet-lined
spaces in a boxwood cabinet.

And with my mother anxious,
almost in tears, at her wits' end,
trying to make sure every
last detail was just right.

All part of the picture, the lamp-lit
dining room, its oval table, red
drapes, polite conversation and
my distraught mother - her melon

and ginger, a Dolly Brown speciality.
Nowadays every supermarket,
every corner shop stocks melons
from Watermelon to Honey Dew -

my mum's speciality no longer
          quite so special.

A memory of summer

Great feedback but
the title escapes me,
Whisper of mortality
What had I been on?
I wonder.

I dredge the poem
from my filing system,
read it silently - in
an instant I am there,
          you too.

Llandaff, a hand-held
stroll in the gathering dark,
stars like gooseberries,
crickets in the hedge, you
          trying to listen.

Black words across
a white page – after all
these years I see your
grey eyes, hear your soft
          Welsh accent.

No photograph can paint
this picture, no video
conjure up this image -
memories packed into
          an 18-line poem.

Party piece

My husband was no cook,
his preferred environment
an office desk, pens
and pencils neatly aligned,
in-tray stacked with files,
each numbered, named,
dates strung on green tags.

As far as he was concerned
a meal wasn't a meal
without potatoes on the side,
baked, roasted, mashed.
From time to time, if I wasn't
around, he'd venture into
kitchen territory to boil a pan
of potatoes, timer in hand.

But he had one party piece
recipe handed down from
mother to son. He'd commandeer
the frying pan, whisk and mix
in secret communion. Tea-towel
over one shoulder, he'd magic up
a tray of spiced Welsh cakes –

not exactly Masterchef, but
pretty damn good for a non-cook.

When you're not there

When, like now,
you're not there –
or here, come to that,
I've had to learn
to live without you.

It's hard, no whisper
of your voice,
no salty smell, empty
mirrors, long-gone
shirts and socks.

When you're not there
I make do with echoes,
the sound of fingers
on bristly chin, a mumbled
I could do with a shave.

A whole new world
now mine – another man,
another bed, different
socks and shirts, another
reflection in the mirror.

This here-and-now man,
like you, can sing in tune,
likes jazz, but he
has a whiskery beard
and yes, I love him.

Fruit for breakfast

It's a bowl I use every day,
shallow, in white and blue,
patterned round the edge
a sea-creature on the base
its out-of-kilter fishy eye
leering up at me.

I stand at the kitchen window
slicing melon into bite-sized
chunks, add cut-up grapes,
green and black, to the mix
to store in the fridge for
tomorrow's breakfast.

He comes up behind me, steals
a bit of melon. *That bowl,* he says,
*we bought it in Singapore, one
of two, it was – until I broke one.
I've always liked it.* A casual
comment. So much I don't know
            about this man.

So much he has to learn about me.

Red shoes

I'd almost forgotten these shoes,
bright red with lowish heels
a touch of anarchy to my otherwise
uninspiring (mainly navy blue)
headmistress outfits.

But last night those same shoes
dominated my dreams. My small
granddaughter, having recently
learned to walk, wobbled about
in my red shoes.

She even tried to climb the stairs,
true to form, refusing adult help,
(she's a very independent child).
There she was in a tiny white dress
        my shoes on her feet.

Brought back memories, me sitting in
my study, complete with red shoes, a group
of unruly boys waiting for a telling-off,
But don't worry, she's very fair, I heard
        one of the old hands say.

What better accolade for any Head?

Promises promises

you promise me
a crocodile
(two turtles
on the side)

in spite of better judgement
I believe you

sort of

a hot day
shadows threading
oak and beech
a lazy river
all rocks and reeds
stitched in sunshine

an unlikely venue
but still I believe you

after all
men make promises
all the time
from *I love you*
downwards

you say
round the next bend
I promise

I imagine
dragon-scales

light-bulb eyes
a snarling smile

who am I to quibble?
they say all things
(even crocodiles)
are possible

and you haven't let me down

yet

Sculptor

(For Rob Kennedy)

He can see pictures
in a block of stone,
walks round it, restless
hand caressing shape,
showing where a head,
the curve of a thigh,
a breast, is hidden.

He can't keep away,
worries it like rosary
beads. His fingers
are eyes probing images
held deep inside, until
he unveils them, chip
by painstaking chip.

Fingertips

like morning rain,
cool, lightweight,
they spill across
my naked body

drifting, pattering,
pinpricks of touch
teasing my skin,
splashing my senses -

for these moments,
I'm my old self,
aware only of
exploratory fingers

making a weather
map of my body,
eyesight unnecessary
touch tantalising as

early morning mist.

Love song

The night icy-dark,
full of bubbling fears
and I thought to myself,
time for a love song,
forgetting for the moment
that I can't sing,
never could hold a tune.

The words flowed
clear through my head,
music on the side, white
notes on a black page:
I love you like raindrops,
I sang, like snowflakes
in winter, a star-beaded sky...

And it made me happy
to sing inside myself,
to feel your stuttering
heart's warm rhythm,
your lazy sex shivering
in my hand, my silent
song soaring into night.

Flatulence

A booming noise from the loo.
'Like World War 3 breaking out,
I shouldn't have had that second
beer,' he says. 'Sorry.' I laugh,
OK it's embarrassing, but
it's what bodies are about.

Sex is wonderful, but it's no
clean-cut business. It's
sweaty, sticky, thoroughly
messy. And as for child-birth,
that's a magical bloody painful
no-holds-barred experience.

We're all animals, cough, spit,
empty our bowels. Sometimes
we get sick, not a pretty sight.
But showered and cleaned up,
a fresh shirt, we're good as new,
ready to dance, flirt, kiss.

I heard a poet, (forgotten his name)
read a piece in tribute to his wife,
'One of the things I miss,' he
said, 'is her tiny gentle fart when
we made love.' A poignant poem,
very beautiful, such a loving detail,

one never to be forgotten.

Nice knowing you

In a dark corner
of the stairway
a man grabs me
in his arms. 'Sorry,'
he whispers, 'So sorry.'

Laughter, shrill chatter,
the usual party sounds
drift upwards. He ignores
his guests, holds me close
'Forgive me?' he asks.

We'd been together
on a casual basis, spent
a couple of nights
in the same bed. Tonight
is his pre-wedding party.

'John!' a woman's voice.
'Where are you?'
'Must go,' he says,
releasing me. A swift
kiss. 'Coming,' he calls.

I follow him downstairs
at a decent interval,
merge into the crowd,
glass of red wine in hand.
Nice knowing you John,

I think to myself.

Pre-owned

You feel a touch chilly,
find a fine woollen stole
in blues and greens
at the back of a drawer.
You wrap it round
your shoulders, shiver,
but soon warm up.

'Nice,' your partner says,
'Where did we buy it?'
'We didn't,' you say.
'It was here already -
one of Barbara's, I guess.'
'Pre-owned - you don't mind?'
Well, not much, you think.

After all, us second-time-
rounders are used to it,
live in pre-owned houses
with pre-owned men. You
draw the line at the bed,
insist on a new one, with
your choice of duvet cover.

You don't have many
old-life possessions, books
of course and memories
crowding in, the smell of him,
a turn of phrase, handwriting
on an odd scrap of paper,
his ring on your left hand.

Your husband, his wife
both gone, where you can't
know. 'How lucky we are,'
you say from time to time
hugging tight to one another
the blue and green stole,
once hers, now yours, safely

back in the bottom drawer.

The witch

'My writing might be illegible,
but I can spell,' I say.
'Like a witch,' he suggests.
I love the idea - reckon
I'd make a pretty good witch.

A tweak here and there,
better weather, fewer floods,
no bush fires or melting ice.
Maybe my spells aren't strong
enough. Start small, I think.

'Sleep well tonight,' and I
sprinkle dream-dust over
his closed eyes, watch, listen
for slowed-down breath, his
body relaxing into sleep-mode.

One down, what now? Any
decent witch has spells to spare
My dodgy eyes - that's asking
too much of an amateur. How
about something less ambitious -

music (about which I know little)
when he sits in with a new band
'Wish me luck,' he says. I do,
wrinkle my nose in the approved
fashion - it works. Generous applause

Perhaps I'm not fluent enough
in witch-speak, need more practice

'How do you spell 'aching', he asks,
I spell it out slowly, *A C H I N G*....
'Thanks,' he says with a nod.

Maybe I should concentrate
on teaching him how to spell,
leave the complicated stuff
to more experienced witches in
the regulation black pointed hats?

Tough cookie

(For Dot)

I've got dementia, she says
with a certain pride. *Tell them,*
she urges her husband. *Tell them
what's wrong with me.* He does,
at length. She's not a well woman.

*It's not all bad. I picked up a man
in the hospital waiting room!*
She smiles in triumph. *True,
I stroked a stranger's arm, mistaking
him for my husband. I did, didn't I?*

She makes light of things, her
frequent falls, her memory lapses,
her tiredness. She's still pretty,
dresses well, smokes the odd
crafty cigarette. This fragile lady

is one tough cookie, wears pride
like bright pink dancing shoes.

We are water

They tell us we're 75%
water. True, poets are
deep wells of words,
words that flow, dribble,
spill, float, swim, drown.

This waterfall of words
lives in my imagination,
flows down A4 pages, spills
on to the computer screen,
sometimes swims into books.

My mother called me
a water baby, at one with
the chilly Scottish waves,
reluctant to come out, even
for towels and a 'chittery bite'.

She didn't know - or care -
that I might drown in words,
that rivers of words would
be my life-line, that I'd
sail on an ocean of poems.

Like everyone else, I am water.

The First Full Moon

Poems by Angie Butler

'For Pete and Cordie in memory of Merryn'

'The cure for anything is salt water, sweat, tears or the sea.'
- Karen Blixen

He is a book

He is a book, the pages turn slowly.
The chapters unfurl at their own pace.

A mystery. No pages may be skipped.

The story keeps changing, yet the characters
stay the same. His plot is not an easy read,

but has a hold on the heart strings.

 Others who have read it, encourage her on.
You'll be glad you kept at it, don't give up just yet.

Keep turning the pages and all will come clear.

It's a hard one, this book, and many have tried it,
but it's one you will treasure

for the rest of your life.

On your mind

So what's going through your mind
as you sit on the stairs,
watching me
as I shower?

The hot water streams down
my naked body,
I turn
and our eyes meet.

Not a word is spoken,
I turn again, soap myself slowly,
and peer at you,
slyly over my shoulder,

through water licked lashes.
You haven't moved,
and continue
to stare unblinking,

until you grow bored,
and walk on
towards the bedroom,
with a flick of your tail.

Heart wrenching

It was a bad line
when they asked for it,

they tested it and took it.
You were dead.

Not a word more
-not a thank you.

So much for organ donors,
just don't ask me again.

Chough

You scream from your hidden ledge
across a pounding memory, teetering feathers
ruffled against the gale. Red shoes, lips.

I glimpse you in the shadows, catch an image
of wheeling wings, below the boiling sadness churns,
moods crash against the bones of cliffs left sobbing.

You won't be silent. You rise up with a voice to drench,
   consume,
pour sorrow from the cliffs of consciousness, the edge,
hiding your realness. Your living amongst us.

I cannot rest, I hear you in the night,
I see your circling sadness.
Tears wash my feet with the incoming tide.

The sounds of the earth

His rheumy eyes spied it, when he rose
to make a cup of tea.
So that's how it happened.
It fitted perfectly into his left ear.

And then he began to notice.
The sounds he had never heard before.
The sounds of the earth.

The cries of joy from the roots when it rained,
and the purrs of pleasure
from the leaves and flowers when the sun shone.
He didn't mention it to anyone.

He kept his remarkable skill and knowledge to himself.
But his wife noticed his contentment,
when he sat back in his chair.

As if he was listening to the most beautiful music.
The most celestial of choirs.
The most secret of dreams of the earth's future.

It had looked like his hearing aid, viewed without his
    glasses.
The sprouting garlic she was going to plant.
They would laugh about it later, when she told him.

Rose

She's a prickly character,
that Rose.
Beautiful I grant you,
looks after herself,

always well turned out
and looks the part.
Her perfume on the wind entraps
you, takes you to another place.

A place of comfort, warmth,
sex even.
But beware, if you know her like I do,
watch her every day, have her in your patch,

you'll keep your distance,
don't delve beneath her lusciousness,
don't try to tame her, have your say.
Don't pick her for your own.

You'll end up with a thorn in your flesh
that can prick, hurt, fester.
And in the end,
result in untold damage

and sleepless nights.

The ring master

The ring master juggles the plates,
he's been here before.
He's really done with this, but needs must
and the show will go on.

His time now spent juggling men, plans, orders,
and customers. They're the worst audience of his craft.
Mind-changing numbness can give him sleepless nights.
They don't get it. It can't be done.

Forget the pretty pictures on the plans, as he scoots
between the acts, checking, firefighting,
mending the trapeze. Making sure
the final show, is a stopper.

His reputation, his audience, his artists, they all expect
from him. He is the biggest performer in the ring.
He is the ring master and the acrobat too, when needed.
The roof rests on his broad shoulders, while his team get on
with their trades.

The ring master juggles the plates,
he's been here before.
He's really done with this, but needs must
and the show will go on.

Secret admirer

Today you balanced
on my rooftop world,
your legs and arms

taking the weight of my future.

You held, you moved,
you swayed,
to another's force,
        in control, in respect, present.

You showed your mastery
and your skill,
you became that leader
        and that king.

Then another day comes,
and more challenges,
more worlds to conquer,
        views to reign over.

More respect to earn,
to lift, and move
and bolt in place,
        more scaffold poles.

Build another day

Take the hammering of sunrise
on sloped lashes,
laid on soft sun stroked cheeks.

Stir the bones of bodies,
warm and leaning to a future together.
Lay down measures suggested,

rules of kindness row on row.
Compliments and thankyous,
cemented in gestures of goodwill.

Construct barriers against sadness
and loss. Protect privacy of concerns
of others with understanding.

Visualize futures of love
to those near you, around you,
across distances, across countries,

and cherish friendship's bonds,
as new found voices sooth
and cling to the laughter of a shared past.

The carpenter

This man whose words seem harsh, his tongue cuts wood,
makes hair for angels, listens to their song.

His looks defy description of a common man.
Yet how he holds himself, brings no concern.

That he is happy with the man he has become.
His father's son, here many would proclaim

and proud he'd be of skills that have remained
and proud his life, his standards are the same.

He fashions ringlets, twisty bits and
wisps of cloud from forests, if they ask.

And nature with such regard and care demands,
that he is prized throughout his land.

He has his rules that he must follow thus
and history from those who choose to tread nearby,

Fools he gladly suffers, but on his terms alone.
If asked for his opinion of his craft, he knows his worth.

And angels clamour for his heavenly touch and
relish too his words that cut.

The woodsman

With skill he sees
the form take place,
his childhood grip,
his body's strength,
his muscle power,
his wield of saw,

all go to make his judgement sure.

He knows this wood,
it framed his life,
as he now frames
it with his knife.
The woodsman
sees his form take place,

he makes my home reflect his grace.

Glass

Men of glass must watch the weather,
feel the squalls and heed the wind.
They work in pairs, one carries another.
The one carried, led reluctantly, not choosing to lead,
better to challenge than be accountable.

Over and over, one leads, one follows,
one watches the weather and heeds the wind,
one feels the squalls and shelters.
Shielding the panes of their life.

Women of glass wait for the storm
to come and the storm to pass,
biding time for the temperature to even,
the seas to calm. They choose their time
to face the waves, then ride and rise

and ride and rise, on the white sea horse
of the falling tide. They steer their boards
and adjust the reins of hope, they overcome
the pains of life and wait again for the storm to pass.

Whitewash

Let's paint over the past.
Let's have a fresh start.
Let's only choose what's going forwards.
Let's cut in, leave bare,
fill the cracks of what suits.

It's the fresh start of dreams.
A new haven,
with a bigger, better view.

Light, comfort, access.
This is what we want.
Let the others decide,
who visits,
who stays, who follows.
We have our hand on the latch.

Bookends

We sit in the window,
like bookends, to our past time's piles,
with books, pamphlets, poetry and papers,
to occupy our hours.

Things to do hang heavy, on landings, corners too,
and sit patiently, tucked away on coffee tables,
out of view of face time
calls from friends afar.

If this is what old age means for us,
I'm happy.
Bring on the years or who decides our ills,
we'll try to keep our fading smiles, however gappy.

And yet that too will have its upside, I am sure,
when other occupations have been shown the door,
and life slows to single living and a carer's chat,
I'm sure by then; I will be sad, but fine with all of that.

So count my blessings is what is said,
daily, on repeat. When sitting in our window,
to occupy the hours.
Bookends together, touching, hands and feet.

Making it

Sex over seventy is
complicated!
The hips,
the knees,
the whistling.

Until the hearing aids are abandoned.

The pills.
Before,   him,
the pills after,   me.
The timing,
the planning.

The day before the grandchildren.
The day after golf,   him
or U3A,   me.

And the post, lengthy nap
Neverthess.......

Sex after seventy

It's surprising, fulfilling,
cautious, thoughtful,
rewarding, intense.

Powerful! All consuming, joyous,
difficult, sensitive, inventive,
memorable, different.

Look forwards to it. Earn it.
Plan for it, think about it,
work at it. Enjoy it. Hugely.

A hidden secret. A select club.
Sex after seventy,
is something to savour.

I promise you.

Old legs

'We treat each other like old legs',
she said, and I knew just what she meant.
Always near each other,
doing the same thing, but differently.

Part of a shared experience,
each looking after its own,
the knees and toes of life,
the bruises of thigh and calf.

Painted nails of joy, meet
summer sandals of satisfaction.
Patted knees of appreciation,
pills suggested in rheumatic understanding.

Old legs in step, aware of each other,
lest one buckle and fall.
A good way to describe a firm friendship,
valued and necessary on this road of life.

Old legs, together,
important to each other,
in the moving on, the living, sharing,
the memories, loss and love.

Supper

You are not a storm in a tea cup
or tangled seaweed hurled on
the beach with the in-coming tide,

nor jewellery cast aside in a maelstrom
of colour, held in a bowl by the mirror.
Nor are you one of the crumpled scarves,

peeping from the dish on a dresser.
coloured, surely, but not in an expensive way,
you are tasteful, and your surface

rocks and rolls, as if you are indeed, a storm
in a tea cup. But no. Instead, you are soup,
that bubbles and warms, cut vegetables

bound in colour, a love that nurtures,
a care that says,
I made this for you. I made you soup.

Come and look at the baby

'Come and look at the baby,
they're coming on Saturday,
he's beautiful, of course,
looks just like his grandad.'

The mask of pleasure,
hides resentment,
despair, sadness.
'Come and look at the baby.'

I'd rather not.

Memory foam

Is it the memory foam
of love that should
be returned to sender?

Does it hold too many false starts,
tiffs, wrong experiences?

Does it sadden your days,
wake your nights of loneliness,
pain your limbs of lust?

Is it the wrong memory foam? Is it
just not suitable, like the girls it has known?

Or perhaps it
is ready for turning,
given a new outlook.

It is awkward I know. Hard to handle,
better with two always,

but not impossible
and always,
always worth a try.

The friend who ate her words

We swap gifts
my friend and I,
made in the early hours of
yesterday.

Slipped into the papers
of memory
and folded
into the bowls of proving,

served cold
in tragedy,
on the broken plates
of sorrow.

We feed each other,
support
each other's
sadness.

With a knowing
and a taste
for words,
food and love.

The first full moon

On this worm moon,
I shall plough my land,
spread goodness on its furrows,
fork in a future for the soil.

On this chaste moon,
I shall reflect, my love
and where it's led,
and where it leads me still.

On this crust moon,
I shall make and share bread,
honour its journey,
value its coming.

On this sap moon,
I will notice the growing,
the life in its veins,
the wind and the rain.

On this death moon,
I will notice the living,
the seasons of life,
and acknowledge every hour.

Your love

Your love folds flat,
fits nicely into
an ordinary handshake.

A greeting so innocent.
Yet feel again, that touch,
somehow right, warm.

The flat of your hand on the pane
as you left. Love,
enough to melt glass.

The smoothing stroke
of an envelope.
The fingering of a stamp.

A hand on hand.
A hand on paper.
A hand on glass.

Our story folded flat,
loved, licked and locked.
We are folded together.

The ladders

Arachne climbed the ladders to Athena's lair,
a throne with crystals hanging there,
she saw, of woven silk, the threads,
adorn the palace, the walls, the beds.

She tiptoed back to her life of toil
and angry thoughts that made her blood boil
'I am just a woman but I have my power.'
She would challenge the goddess and make her cower.

'I'm the better at weaving, despite her birth,
I'll show her who's best,' she uttered the curse.
The words were said – like a splash of blood,
she would win at weaving, she knew she could.

But when she turned, Athena was there,
and the contest began, to prove the dare.
And weave they did, as night went to day.
Who would win the bet? Who would have their say?

The end came then, like sun entering cloud
and the face of Athena bore the mark of a shroud.
'You like climbing ladders - you dare to climb mine,
you think you can weave child, I give you this sign.'

She tapped with her spindle; she tapped the floor thrice.
'Lest others try too, just let them think twice,
you will weave your own ladders, for evermore,
you will cower, you will shrivel, you will live on the floor.'

'How dare you think you can challenge my worth?
Those ladders of power beat the power of your curse.'

And so to this day, she builds ladders with skill
and her life depends on her power to kill.

Arachne makes ladders, she weaves her own lair.
When seen, others curse her, rain crystals hang there.
They see of woven silk, the threads
adorn the hedges, the walls, the beds.

Haiku thread

Take the wool of words.
Start knitting into your shape.
Unravel problems.

Out in the garage

Out in the garage there's a pile of vinyl records,
waiting to find a home,
Bought by my parents with tightly held shillings,
they conjure memories, every one.

Some went to a friend, where her husband will play
them at festivals, and people will smile and dance.
But this Spring I select six, and hold them tight,
they are ready to take flight.

Their labels green, blue and yellow, glow.
They are just the thing for the birthday
of an old dear friend, and will bring back
special memories for him too.

The records slip one by one,
not onto a turn table, but into
the oven, balanced on a plant pot.
and magic happens.

The melted folding shapes held carefully
are pulled to form a bowl,
filled with compost and three hyacinth bulbs.
My childhood memories,

unearth the music of Spring.

The map

Her looks are deceptive, but get close enough
to open her up, this small map has detail and information.
She has all the right roads to follow
and she can be like a beacon lighting
a path, a lifeline, for anyone lost.

She is many countries and is understood in them all.
Different languages are no problem to her,
in fact, she relishes learning new ways,
understanding cultures and sharing the right paths.
Hills and valleys show without effort,

woods and mountains put a shine on her face,
a quality, which reflects how far she and
others have come. But it is the places on the coast,
where she comes into her own. Her salt licked
surface and sea breezes gently lift her.

She's strong enough
not to crumble in the toughest of storms
and the worst of weather too. This is a map
that pushes boundaries. Relishes detail.
Overcomes problems and helps others find their way.

No one should be without a map
            like her.

Quality

It's the adverts,
we're watching the football,
I stare at the box of chocolates.
The descriptions on the lid are set out in three rows of five.
Each one the same, but each one different
in size and colour. The box is nearly empty.

And now number fifteen. Today, still wrapped
under her silver foil, hidden, tempting. Will this one
be the favourite, even when the chocolate's licked off?
Will this one last any longer than the nutty one,
the one too sweet, the one too hard, not quite right,
or just not to his taste?

When the silver foil slithers to the floor, will the taste
linger for a life time, be the favourite of the box
or leave him wanting more?
We keep each wrapper safe, even when he's thrown
them away. The tastes will always linger in our mouths,
as we reclaim his discarded treats.

Our son's hand hovers over the box
as he makes his choice.
The lid held open before shutting.

Moving on!

I'll miss your groans when I try to turn you on
in the mornings, the wait for you to wake up slowly,
stare at me with blinking eye, holding messages
I could not hope to read. I'd wait for you; busy myself
with other thoughts, until you were ready.

Then, without moving, every fibre of your body
would be alive, every touch electric, wanting more.
You made me unstoppable. My fingers caressed your
faithful frame, solid, dependable. Twenty years by my side,
you have been there, what was mine was yours.

We have shared much. I have wept over your
tear stained letters. You have listened patiently
as I have gone over my pain, shared my three o'clock
nightmares, waited till the words were right to let go. You
have given me your power and knowledge without
question.

I will miss what we had together. Others did not understand
our bond. There are things only you and I understood.
I know you're there should I need you. But for today,
I'm leaving you and going to my new, very smart,
uncomplaining and quite responsive,

laptop.

Evil comes

Evil comes with many heads,
it comes with a nod and a wink,
a gift. It comes whispering silently,
floating on the winds of thought,
flying on the wings of feathers.

Evil can float distances,
or fall at your feet unnoticed.
It sets roots down,

sends tendrils searching for gaps,
where poison can leak.
It spreads and grows.
It spawns danger,
carries heavy loads with easy strength,

gathers followers.
Holds up its hands to interrogation,
courts argument,

with truth and lies equally.
Speaks into the air with a smile.
It can wait. Bide its time to invade.

But I know where it lives.

Clearing out

The month's teasing windows
open a crack, some flung, wide as wide,
as my mother's thrifty necklaces,
trickle through memory fingers.
The air, the wind, the gales of thoughts
power in, flow through, whirl around.

The sudden gusts of
overwhelming sadness
come from nowhere, shout at the calm,
shatter the peaceful minutes,
roar at the sunshine, make chaos
out of order. Deny the task.

Later, through another window,
life and laughter come
and the chuckle of the knowing wind
and the memory of music
of another time. Lends a hand
to choose the next destination.

Garden nasturtiums

Your nodding, smiling blush, cheers me
on this grey, wet, insistent day.

You stretch your searching arms,
across the glistening, shiny, garden paving,

reach out to guide my eyes to lush leaves
languishing in summer rain.

Your flat round hands like Amazon
tongues lolling, catch every rain drop,

and guide life down grooved stems
to waiting thirsty earth.

With this liquid power and
tomorrow's promised warmth,

another stem, another flower
will greet me when I wake,

and trailing fingers once again
will brush my eager feet.

Camping in July

Blown to the sky with a godly breath, as if
each seed from this place, leaves its hidden
landscape, to shine above and show its power.

If every seed from every plant,
like the stars, shone, the reflection would mean
the earth and sky were joined.

A single candlelight wipes out the beauty
of a million years, when contemplation of this
universe becomes too much for my human frame,

cocooned in its downy bag
and canvas wrap.
I leave one hell for another.

From my world of noise and death to
a world of silence and infinity. Your hand on the match,
saves me from those thoughts of heaven.

Writer's nest

I sit, this bird who writes,
in a nest of paper.
Colours? Usually bright,

yellow, and of course, white,
but with a dash of blue too.
Here and there,

post it notes float to the floor
with wise words, lest I forget and more,
to be penned, getting to the core

of thoughts, hopes and dreams, there's reams
of paper, pictures too, that line my nest,
my home, my comfort,

my inspiration and my rest.
My nest is high up, with views to the west,
over the trees, to the sea, that's where I love to be.

The weather means nothing to me
but if asked, honestly,
what I like to see

is a soft gentle mist and a cat on my knee
and a light grey sky to write by,
and a man asleep, not far away,

so I can peck at my nest
and rearrange words my way
without another having a say.

And fuss and fiddle
to my hearts delight,
at home in my nest

where the world seems right,
amid bits of paper, usually white,
and totally like a bird

who can write.

The voice

The voice of reason
haunts me, shadows
my every move,
tries to walk in my shoes.
The voice of reason doesn't see
the view I see, needs explanation,
stops the inspiring new,
closes the curtains against the light.

The voice of reason,
latches the door
against exciting opportunities,
is wary of the draft of possibility,
won't climb the ladder,
to see the view, chokes my song,
can't see the right,
highlights the wrong.

The voice of reason
has my back,
lifts me up when I'm down,
is what I sometimes lack.
The voice of reason,
sometimes is right,
and calms
my restless night.

Moira Andrew

I was born and educated in Scotland. I became a primary teacher, married, had two daughters and was so busy just keeping things going at home and at school, that there was little time to try my hand at writing. I divorced, became a lecturer in Craigie College of Education in Ayr and began writing poetry, enjoying making words work for me.

My next job was as head of a primary school near Bristol and it was there that I started to write for children. After all, it's hardly fair to ask children to write a poem if you're not prepared to put your own words and ideas on the line. And believe me, primary children are the sternest of critics!

When I remarried, I moved to Wales, left full-time teaching and started a new career as a freelance writer. I'm lucky to be able to combine my teaching experience and interest in artwork and display with my love of writing. I have a number of books in publication, mostly those intended for use by primary school teachers. My first and possibly most successful is 'Language in Colour', published by Belair Publications Ltd. although my personal favourite is 'Paint a Poem', also from Belair.

After my lovely husband Allen died in 2003, I moved to Cornwall where I lived for ten years with my cat Bonnie. Although I visited fewer schools, I worked in the schoolroom of the RCH Hospital (Treliske) in Truro where the pupils were patients. This was an exciting and thoroughly worthwhile project – one that I now miss.

85

In 2005 I joined the prestigious Falmouth Poetry Group. The standard of my poetry came on by leaps and bounds and I made many friends among the members. I also set up the Cornish Chapter of the Society of Authors. I had two poetry collections published during my time in Cornwall, 'This Year, Next Year', and 'Firebird' (IDP).

In 2013 I moved to Nunney, a village near Frome to live with Norman, a teaching colleague from the 80s – before I met Allen! We spend part of the year in Norman's house in Cyprus, enjoy jazz, (Norman has his own band: The New Academic Feetwarmers). I'm now a member of the Frome Writers' Collective and I've set up a new poetry-writing group. Of course, I continue to write! Poets don't give up easily! My current publishers are Poetry Space, 'Wish a Wish' and Indigo Dreams Publishing, 'Man in the Moon'.

www.moiraandrew.com

Angie Butler

I'm a poet, writer and teacher from Cornwall. My highlights include holding the Guinness Book of Records for the largest gathering of pirates, my reading of 'Chough' being Pick of the Week for Radio 4, and performing my story 'Bodelva' with six hundred children playing instruments, to music composed for me, with the Bournemouth Symphony Orchestra for the 10th anniversary of the Eden Project and also being asked to work on books about The Land Army, The Jubilee Pool and Seasonality and Healthy Living.

I have written and held drama workshops about myths and legends, especially giants, worked for Hospital Radio on the children's ward, been a founder member of The Pz Lit Fest and initiated many fund raising poetry competitions. Latterly I've taught in Kenya while visiting an orphanage in my daughter's memory. My father, grandfather and two uncles were vicars from South Wales and I hope I can continue the legacy of those who 'wrote and spoke', with empathy. I feel that 'to inspire writing, gives a life time of freedom and leaves a legacy of ink.'

Moira Andrew is an admired inspirational mentor and friend.

www.westcountrygiants.co.uk

Published by
www.publishandprint.co.uk

Printed in Great Britain
by Amazon

63207369R00058